A boy called Jesus

A boy called Jesus

A Popjustice Book
Illustrated by David Whittle

First published in Great Britain in 2007 by Friday Books
An imprint of The Friday Project Limited
83 Victoria Street, London SW1H 0HW

www.thefridayproject.co.uk
www.fridaybooks.co.uk

ISBN – 13   978 1 905548 40 8

British Library Cataloguing in Publication Data

A catalogue record for this book is available
from the British Library

Designed and produced by Staziker Jones
www.stazikerjones.co.uk

The Publisher's policy is to use paper
manufactured from sustainable sources

This book belongs to

I am ____ years old

My favourite Jesus story is ——————

When I grow up, I want to be ——————

Here is my autograph

This is Jesus.

Jesus is a very famous boy who was born a very long time ago. He is older than your granny and your grandpa – put together!

He died a long time ago but he is not really dead, although he lives in Heaven with people who ARE dead.

Jesus has a beard.

Before you read this you should know that there is another book you can buy which is all about the story of Jesus.

Unfortunately the other book takes a very long time to read. It was written a long time ago, uses complicated words, and because lots of people worked on it is quite confusing.

People say it is a good book but the one you are holding now has pictures in it so is better.

Some people think that what you will read in this book is not true. They think that just because there are dinosaur bones in the ground it proves that Jesus did not exist. They think it is more likely that people used to be made out of fish!

People who think the story is true think that dinosaurs did not exist and that the bones in the ground are not important. They think that people like you and I were just invented one day by Jesus' dad.

Both stories seem quite far-fetched but if you think about it one of them is bound to be true. Let's imagine for the time being that dinosaurs did not exist.

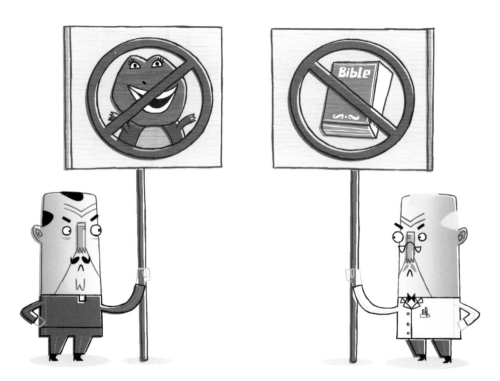

Jesus has a very famous and powerful dad.
Jesus' dad is called God.

Jesus would not be famous if it were not for
his father, which means he is a bit like Peaches
Geldof or Paris Hilton.

But Peaches Geldof is good at playing records
in nightclubs and Paris Hilton sings some songs,
so what is it that makes Jesus so special?

Well, while he was on Earth, Jesus had special powers. Would you like to have special powers? Imagine your packed lunch: you could turn a boring bottle of water into a Capri Sun, or turn five packets of Cheese Strings into enough Cheese Strings for your entire school!

But as well as being like Peaches Geldof and Paris Hilton, Jesus was also a bit like Spider-Man, because he knew that with great power came great responsibility. He did not perform magic tricks just to show off, like that silly David Blaine.

Instead he would perform tricks to let people know he was special and that his famous dad was who he said he was.

slurp

Jesus was born in a little town called Bethlehem. Jesus' daddy, God, put the little baby Jesus into the tummy of a girl called Mary.

Normally you have to kiss someone for a baby to appear in your belly but Mary had not kissed her husband, Joseph. Joseph should have been annoyed but he knew this was alright though because a ghost had told him the whole, long story in a dream!

Jesus was born in a shed which smelt of donkey poo. The ghost also told Joseph that the baby should be called Jesus, so they didn't have to think of a name.

As soon as Jesus was born, people began to realise that he was special.

An angel told some shepherds, who then told the news to everyone else. Don't ever trust a shepherd with a secret!

Wise men went to say hello to baby Jesus as well. They took him presents and because they were wise they did not take him anything with sharp spikes, small parts or bags which were a potential suffocation hazard.

One person who did want to give Jesus something with a sharp spike was King Herod.

King Herod was a mean man who was jealous of how much everyone liked Jesus.

'KILL THE LITTLE BABY JESUS OR ANYONE WHO MIGHT BE HIM!!!' Herod roared.

Fortunately the people who were supposed to kill Jesus decided not to because of ghosts in their dreams.

Jesus became a carpenter.

He made things out of wood.

When he was grown up, Jesus met a boy called John. John sort of knew Jesus' famous dad and immediately recognised Jesus. 'Behold!' he said, waving his arms around, 'It's the lamb of God!'.

God appeared in the sky and said, 'This is my son, in whom I am well pleased'. God talked like he was in *EastEnders* but he was allowed to because he was God and what he said went.

Jesus decided to go to the desert for forty days to get his head together.

'ARGHRGHRHRHRGHGH!!!!!!' roared The Devil.

The Devil knew Jesus' dad from way back. They did not get on.

'AGHRGHRHRGRGH!!!' roared the Devil for a second time. 'Why don't you sack off all this "being good" business and come and be nasty with me in Hell for all eternity?'

'No thanks,' said Jesus.

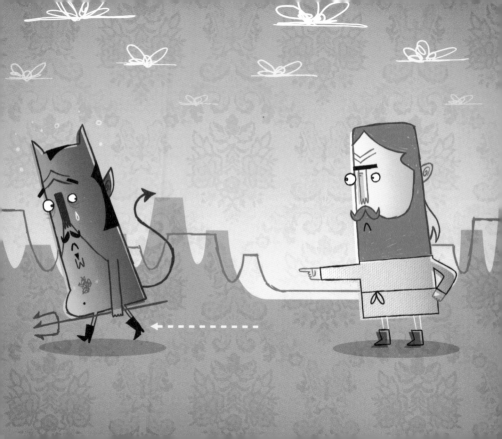

Jesus had a bit of a think about what he was doing on Earth. It is sometimes hard if you have a famous dad to prove that you are a good person in your own right. To make matters worse, Jesus was thirty. He did not have a wife or any children. He was at a crossroads.

He decided to become a special teacher. Because it was a long time ago and Jesus was not teaching in an inner city school, his class size was quite small and he only had twelve people to teach.

They were called disciples.

One day Jesus took his disciples onto a mountainside and said lots of important things about how important it is to be nice to other people.

Even if you do not believe a single word of this story, that is quite a good rule to live your life by.

Big crowds gathered and they all agreed with him. It was like when your teacher stands up in assembly at the end of term and tells you that you've all done very well but that you have to carry on doing well in the future as well.

Jesus was very popular. This upset some important people who decided it would be better if Jesus were dead.

Unfortunately for those nasty people, everyone loved Jesus so much that they could not find anyone who wanted to kill him!

It is lucky this was in the days before the phrase 'if a job is worth doing, it's worth doing yourself' was invented.

One day Jesus had a dinner party.

For the starter he gave his guests some bread.
'This is my body!' said Jesus.

For a drink, Jesus poured some wine. 'This is my blood!'
he said.

If you are at a dinner party you have to be polite
and take what you are given, even if someone is
telling you it is their blood and guts.

During a lull in conversation at the dinner, Jesus lightened the mood by telling his twelve guests that one of them would betray him.

It was a bit like an episode of *Big Brother*!

After dinner, Jesus went to the diary room for a pray.

When Jesus had finished praying his friend Judas, who had been at the dinner party, turned up.

'Hello Judas!' said Jesus.

'Hello Jesus,' said Judas.

Judas had brought some people with him, who arrested Jesus.

Jesus made a mental note not to invite Judas to any more dinner parties.

Jesus was in trouble for saying that he was the son of God. In spite of all Jesus' magic tricks, the people in charge thought that Jesus was lying and that Jesus should be punished.

The people in charge thought the best way of dealing with it was to nail Jesus to a cross and let him die.

It was very sad.

Once Jesus was dead, his body was placed in a big cave, but when someone went to check up on the cave a few days later Jesus' body was gone!

Instead of thinking that someone had probably stolen it or that it had been stolen by a bear or something, it was decided that Jesus had come back to life.

This made people less sad.

Nowadays, Jesus lives in Heaven with his dad.

People who believe all this think that one day he might come back to Earth. If he does, people will probably not believe him when he says he is the son of God. Again!

But instead of nailing him to a cross they'll probably try to lock him up in a mental asylum, or perhaps he'll end up as a popstar or TV presenter instead.

This is Jesus. Who's this with him? Oh dear – it's Judas!

Cut out around the dots (ask a grown-up to help!)
and wrap Jesus and Judas around your fingers
to act out special scenes!

Jesus: I suppose I will have to forgive
you for all that funny business.
Judas: I knew you'd have to do that!
Jesus: I know you knew.
Judas: HA HA HA.

Hours of fun!

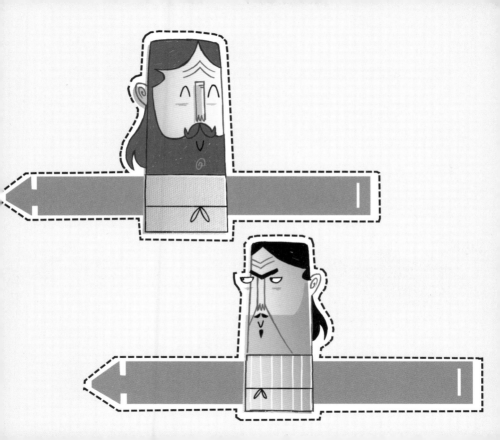

Popjustice.com is the greatest pop website on the face of Planet Earth. We update every day with the best pop stuff.

Drop in at **www.popjustice.com/idols** for downloadable wallpapers, screensavers and other random nonsense.

Why not send us an email? idols@popjustice.com